The Life and Work of
Michelangelo
Buonarroti

Richard Tames

Heinemann Library
Chicago, Illinois

© 2001, 2006 Heinemann Library
a division of Reed Elsevier Inc.
Chicago, Illinois

Customer Service 888-454-2279
Visit our website at www.heinemannraintree.com

Designed by Jo Malivoire and Q2A Creative
Printed in China by South China Printing Company

10 09 08 07 06
10 9 8 7 6 5 4 3 2 1

New edition ISBN: 1-40348-494-5 (hardcover)
              1-40348-505-4 (paperback)

The Library of Congress has cataloged the first edition as follows:
Tames, Richard
        Michelangelo Buonarotti / Richard Tames.
            p. cm. — (The life and work of–)
        Includes bibliographical references and index.
        Summary: A biography of the Renaissance sculptor, painter, architect, and poet,
    including a list of places where his art can be seen today.
            ISBN 1-57572-343-3
            1. Michelangelo Buonarotti, 1475-1564--Juvenile literature. 2.
        Artists-Italy-Biography-Juvenile literature. [1. Michelangelo Buonarotti, 1475-1564.
        2. Artists.] I. Title. II. Series.

N6923.B9 T36   2000
709'.2—dc21   00-025785
            CIP

Acknowledgments
The author and publishers are grateful to the following for permission to reproduce copyright material: Archivi Alinari: pp. 5, 9, 11, 13, 15, 21; Archivio Buonarroti: p. 27; Bridgeman Art Library: Casa Buonarroti, Florence p. 7, Vatican Museums and Galleries, Italy p. 17; E T Archive: p. 28; J Allan Cash Ltd: p. 23; Photo RMN: R G Ojeda p. 19; Robert Harding Picture Library: Simon Harris p. 25; Scala, Museo dellí Opera del Duomo: p. 29

Cover: *Pietà* by Michelangelo Buonarroti, reproduced by permission of Bridgeman Art Library.

The publishers would like to thank Nancy Harris for her assistance in the preparation of this book.

Some words in this book are in bold, **like this.** You can find out what they mean by looking in the Glossary.

Contents

Who was Michelangelo?

Michelangelo was a great artist. He thought of himself as a **sculptor**. A sculptor carves wood or stone to make art. He was also a painter, a poet, and an **architect**.

In Michelangelo's time most art was made for churches. Michelangelo's painting of God giving life to Adam is on the ceiling of the Sistine **Chapel** in Rome, Italy.

The Pupil

Michelangelo was born on March 6 1475 in Caprese, Italy. His family moved to Florence a few weeks after he was born. At school he wanted to become a painter. The rich Medici family let him **study** the works of art they owned.

Michelangelo became interested in
sculpture, too. He was only 16 when he
carved this sculpture of the baby Jesus
with his mother, Mary.

The Student

Michelangelo wanted to understand how the human body worked. He **studied** human bodies in a hospital in Florence. This helped him make his paintings and **sculptures** look real.

Michelangelo also studied the work of other artists. He made his own drawings of **frescoes**, such as this one by the Italian artist Masaccio. This taught him about the use of color and **perspective**.

Fame

Michelangelo moved to Rome in 1496.
He carved a **statue** of Jesus lying dead in
Mary's arms. This statue made him famous.

The statue was for a church. It is called the *Pietà*. The two figures are very different. One is dead, one is alive. One is a man, one is a woman. Michelangelo carved it from a single piece of stone.

Working in Florence

In 1501 Michelangelo returned to Florence. He began work on a **statue** of David for the city's **cathedral**. David is a hero in the Bible.

Michelangelo's statue of David became famous. People thought it showed what a perfect human being would look like.

The Pope's Tomb

In 1505 Michelangelo planned a huge **tomb** for **Pope** Julius II, in Rome. But Michelangelo often took on more work than he had time to do. He never finished making the tomb.

The tomb was going to have more than 40 **statues** on it. This one of **Moses** was meant to go in the middle. Moses looks very real—even down to his sandals.

The Sistine Chapel

In 1508 **Pope** Julius II asked Michelangelo to paint the ceiling of the Sistine **Chapel** in Rome. Michelangelo did not really want to do it. He liked working on **sculptures** better.

It took Michelangelo four years to paint
the ceiling. The paintings tell stories
from the Bible. They are some of the
most famous paintings in the world.

Cities at War

Italy was often at war during Michelangelo's lifetime. In 1528 and 1529 he worked on plans for buildings and walls to protect Florence during an attack.

Michelangelo made this **sketch** in 1528. It shows his plans for the defense of Florence. He wanted ditches to be dug all around the city.

Working for the Medici

From 1515 until 1534 Michelangelo worked for the Medici family in Florence. He **designed** a **chapel**, a library, two **tombs**, and a grand house for them.

This is one of the tombs Michelangelo
designed for the Medici family. The two
figures at the front are meant to be
Dawn and Dusk.

Back to Rome

In 1534 Michelangelo moved to Rome.
He **designed** a new square for the center
of the city.

Michelangelo redesigned the old city hall in Rome. He also designed these special floor patterns for the ground with a **statue** at the center.

The Pope's Architect

In 1546 Michelangelo became the **Pope's** main **architect**. He worked on the great church of St Peter in Rome.

Michelangelo **designed** the **dome**
of St Peter's. Sadly he died before
it was finished.

Last Years

From 1546 to 1547 Michelangelo **designed** a palace for the relatives of **Pope** Paul III to live in. He also wrote many poems and letters to his friends and family.

Michelangelo was left-handed and he had beautiful handwriting. Many of his poems are about love, even though he never got married.

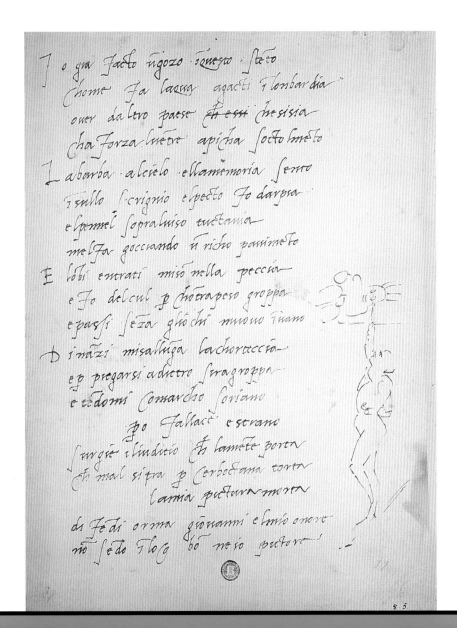

Michelangelo Dies

Michelangelo died on February 18 1564. He was 88 years old. He was buried in Florence. His **tomb** was **designed** by a pupil of his named Giorgio Vasari.

This is part of a **statue** Michelangelo was making for his own tomb. He never finished it. It shows Michelangelo himself, when he was 75 years old.

Timeline

1475	Michelangelo Buonarroti is born in Caprese, Italy on March 6.
1488	Michelangelo trained with the artist Ghirlandaio.
1490–92	Michelangelo lives in the Medici Palace.
1496	Michelangelo moves from Florence to Rome.
1501–04	Michelangelo carves the **statue** of David.
1508–12	Michelangelo paints the ceiling of the Sistine **Chapel**.
1528–29	Michelangelo **designs** defenses for Florence.
1534	Michelangelo leaves Florence for the last time.
1534–41	Michelangelo paints a **fresco** (*The Last Judgement*) for a wall in the Sistine Chapel.
1546	Michelangelo becomes the **Pope's** main **architect**.
1550	Giorgio Vasari writes the first biography of Michelangelo.
1564	Michelangelo Buonarroti dies on February 18.

Glossary

architect person who designs buildings

cathedral large and important church

chapel small church or part of a bigger church or cathedral

design to think of an idea or plan and put it on paper

dome rounded roof

fresco painting done on wet plaster so the color soaks in

Moses Bible hero, who was given the stones with the Ten Commandments by God

perspective way of drawing to show how far away things are

Pope leader of the Roman Catholic Church

sculptor person who carves wood or stone to make works of art

sculpture statue or carving

sketch another word for a drawing

statue carved, molded, or sculpted figure of a person or animal

study learn about a subject

tomb place to be buried in

More Books to Read

Wolfe, Gillian. *Oxford First Book of Art.* New York: OUP, 2004.

More Paintings to See

The Holy Family, Museum of Fine Arts, Boston, Mass.

Studies for the Libyan Sibyl, 1508-12. Metroplitan Museum of Fine Art, New York City, N.Y.

Index